Dedication

For the parents who keep showing up, even when it's hard, and for the children whose emotions speak louder than words.

When you calm the storm inside, connection becomes the cure.

Decoding Hidden Messages and Creating Connections That Heal

8 PRINCIPLES FOR UNDERSTANDING EMOTIONALLY COMPLEX KIDS

KIMBERLEY CLAYTON BLAINE, MA, LMFT

ISBN: 979-8-9935610-4-2

Contents

Introduction

Emotionally complex kids aren't broken, spoiled, or intentionally oppositional. They are children whose nervous systems run deep, causing them to feel everything, question everything, and react to life with an intensity that others may find confusing or overwhelming. But beneath their big emotions and behaviors is a brilliant brain trying to make sense of a world that often moves too fast for its own sensitivity.

As a therapist, I've sat with hundreds of these sweet, emotionally charged kids, and their parents, who walk into my office exhausted, misunderstood, and quietly afraid they're doing it all wrong. Parents often tell me, "Nothing seems to work," or "Why does everything turn into a battle?" But the truth is, these kids aren't giving their parents a hard time; they're *having* a hard time.

This book is an invitation to look below the surface, to understand what your child is really trying to tell you through their behavior. Because every outburst, every shutdown, and every refusal hides a message about emotional safety, connection, and meaning. When we learn to decode those messages, we stop reacting to behavior and start responding to the child *within* the behavior.

Each of the eight principles in this book offers a new lens for understanding your emotionally complex child. You'll learn how play builds emotional architecture, why "defiance" can signal moral growth, how to anticipate dysregulation before it happens, and how your own nervous system can become your child's most powerful tool for healing. You'll learn that emotional development doesn't end in childhood; it continues in you, too.

This isn't a manual for "managing" kids. It's a guide for growing alongside them, for co-regulating, decoding, and deepening your connection in ways that repair and rewire the brain through relationship.

So, take a deep breath, and set aside the parenting advice that tells you to fix, punish, or control.

Here, you'll learn to see differently, listen beyond just words, and respond with compassion instead of control. Because when you begin to understand your emotionally complex child, you change not only their world but also your own.

Chapter One

When Nature and Nurture Intertwine: Raising Your Brilliant Little Human

Every child is born with a story already written in their cells, one passed down through generations, coded in their DNA. You can see it in their eyes, their gestures, their temperament, and sometimes even in their struggles. It's easy to forget, but you handed your child a biological legacy before you ever taught them a single word.

We often say things like, "She gets that from me," or "He's just like his father." And it's true: our genetic makeup is potent and powerful. It influences everything from how our children respond to stress, to their sensitivity to sound, to how quickly they recover from disappointment. But here's the good news: genetics are not destiny.

The Dance of Nature and Nurture

Think of DNA as the foundation of a house, and nurture as the design, décor, and daily care that turn a house into a home. The blueprint may set the limits of the structure, but what you do inside those walls determines how livable and loving it becomes.

Your child's temperament, their baseline energy, curiosity, adaptability, and emotional intensity, is a reflection of that genetic foundation. Maybe your child is cautious like you were or impulsive like your brother. Maybe they need order and routine to feel safe, or perhaps they crave novelty and risk. These traits don't appear by accident.

However, what you *do* with those traits, how you respond, model, and shape experiences, can either amplify their strengths or deepen their struggles.

For example:

- A child with a naturally anxious temperament who grows up with calm, consistent caregivers may become cautious yet confident, learning that the world is safe and predictable.
- That same child, raised in chaos or inconsistency, might grow into an adult who constantly scans for danger, never fully trusting calm moments.

Nurture doesn't erase nature; it partners with it.

Twelve Important Years

Research suggests that the first twelve years of life are when nurture holds its greatest influence. During these years, your child's brain is extraordinarily malleable, wiring itself through every experience, tone of voice, touch, and relationship.

From birth to twelve, you are the architect, the emotional translator, and the teacher of what it means to be human. These years are your window for shaping empathy, moral understanding, and resilience. It's when your child learns:

- What love feels like in the nervous system
- How to manage frustration without shame
- How to stay connected even when they feel angry or afraid

While children are little, cooperation often comes more easily. There's an underlying ease when you say, "Time for bed," or "Let's go," and they follow along without too much resistance. Their sense of identity is still developing, and they want to please you and stay close to you. You are, in many ways, their entire world.

But as they approach the tween years, roughly ages ten to twelve, that landscape begins to shift dramatically. Their brain is entering a massive remodeling phase, pruning unused connections and building new ones to prepare them for adulthood. Hormones surge. Peer opinions start to carry more weight. They begin to think critically, question authority, and crave independence.

Neurobiologically, they are becoming mini-adults, highly perceptive, emotionally reactive, and wickedly clever. This is when getting your child to "do what you say" starts to feel impossible. They can out-argue you, outmaneuver you, and see right through inconsistencies. They are testing boundaries, not to defy *you*, but to define *themselves.*

This shift can be jarring for parents who have enjoyed years of relatively smooth cooperation. Suddenly, every request feels like a debate, and every reminder turns into a negotiation. But this isn't failure; it's growth. It's the brain's way of moving from dependency to autonomy.

That being said, bracing yourself for this stage is essential. You'll need to stay calm, cool, collected, and compassionate, all while holding steady boundaries. When you stay emotionally grounded, you communicate safety, even when their emotions feel big or chaotic.

Remember, this is not the time to tighten control but to strengthen connection. Your tween doesn't need a commander. Instead, they need a calm, confident guide who can hold both authority and empathy in the same breath.

By age twelve, the scaffolding of identity is largely built. From that point forward, peers, teachers, and the social world start to play a much stronger role in refining and testing that structure. Your voice doesn't disappear, but it becomes part of a chorus.

So when your middle schooler rolls their eyes and insists you "don't understand," it's not rejection but neurological independence in action. Their brain is expanding, experimenting, and building a sense of self that must eventually stand apart from you. It's frustrating, yes, but it's also developmentally normal.

Your Influence Is Never Lost

Even though the power of nurture changes after twelve, it never fully vanishes. Your child's brain keeps track of the emotional tone you bring into the room. Your regulation becomes their inner voice. Your compassion becomes the model for how they treat themselves. And your boundaries become the blueprint for what they later accept in relationships.

So, while their friends may influence how they dress, what they listen to, or what they say, *you still shape who they become.* Your job simply evolves, from direct sculptor to quiet anchor.

Knowing Yourself to Know Your Child

Understanding your own DNA lens gives you insight into your child's. If you were the sensitive one, you may now be raising a sensitive child. If you were the dreamer who had trouble finishing things, you might recognize that spark in your child, too.

Rather than trying to "fix" what mirrors you, try to observe it with curiosity. Ask yourself:

- Is this trait truly a problem or just an echo of my own wiring?
- What did I need when I was this age?
- How can I guide my child in ways I wish I had been guided?

Parenting from awareness rather than fear turns generational patterns into opportunities for growth. It helps you respond to your child's behavior as communication, not confrontation.

The Gift of Knowing the Timeline

Knowing that nurture has a window of strongest impact doesn't mean you should panic; it means you can be intentional. You have twelve powerful years to build a foundation of safety, belonging, and trust that will outlast every teenage storm and every college heartbreak.

When you show up consistently, regulate yourself before reacting, and speak to your child with empathy, you're not just teaching skills; you're shaping brain pathways that support lifelong resilience.

The gift is knowing that what you do *now* matters deeply, and the challenge is doing it with patience and presence.

And the reward? Watching your brilliant little human become the adult you always hoped they'd be, one who can love, lead, and live with courage and heart.

Decode Message

Your child's behavior often reflects both their genetic wiring and the environment you create for them. When you see a familiar trait, stubbornness, sensitivity, perfectionism, pause before labeling it as a flaw. It might be your child showing you a piece of your own DNA in motion.

Decoded: *"I'm becoming who I'm wired to be. Please help me learn to use it well."*

Recognize the shared threads between you and your child not as burdens but as blueprints. What you once struggled with, you now have a second chance to heal, through them and for them.

 Connection Moment

Sit quietly and think of one trait your child has that feels familiar, something you share.

Now, instead of focusing on how it frustrates you, ask yourself:

- How did this trait serve me when I was young?
- How could it become my child's strength if it's nurtured well?

Then, tell your child something like, "You know, I see a lot of myself in you when you (name the behavior). I used to feel that way, too. Let's figure out how we can make that work *for* you instead of *against* you."

That simple reflection is more powerful than any lecture. It tells your child: *We're on the same team. I understand you, not because I've studied you, but because I am part of you.*

Chapter Two

The Hard Work of Play: Core Architecture of Emotion, Language, and Thought

If childhood had a job description, the title would be simple: *Play.*

Play is not frivolous. It's not what children do once the "real work" of learning is done. It *is* the work of learning, feeling, thinking, and becoming.

Children are the CEOs of curiosity. They invent, experiment, destroy, rebuild, and imagine entire worlds in the span of an afternoon. Through play, the brain learns to sequence events, make meaning, regulate emotions, and form relationships. In fact, play is the primary operating system for growth.

Why Play Is the Work of Childhood

Since children don't yet have to enter the workforce, play becomes their daily practice for life. It's how they rehearse for the complex world they'll one day navigate. When we see play as "just fun," we miss the invisible architecture it's building underneath: the wiring for language, empathy, attention, and creativity.

A child pretending to be a teacher is rehearsing leadership.

A child lining up cars is organizing the world into patterns, stability, and self-soothing predictable scenes.

A child negotiating turn-taking is learning diplomacy.

Every giggle, squabble, and imaginary scenario is scaffolding for emotional intelligence.

Solo Play: The Art of Inner Creativity

Solo play is the birthplace of imagination. It allows children to create without judgment, to problem solve independently, and to find pleasure in their own company.

A child building with blocks alone is learning perseverance.

A child drawing for an hour in silence is building focus and self-expression.

A child talking quietly to their stuffed animals is experimenting with language, tone, storytelling, and self-empowerment.

Solo play nurtures *emotional regulation* because the child learns to tolerate frustration ("The tower fell, but I can rebuild it"), to feel mastery, and to self-soothe.

Emotionally complex kids especially need solo play. It offers refuge from overstimulation and provides a safe space to process feelings at their own pace.

Peer Play: The Laboratory of Empathy

When children play with peers, they enter one of the most important emotional classrooms of their lives.

Through peer play, kids learn to:

- **Negotiate:** "You be the dragon, and I'll be the knight."
- **Cooperate:** "Let's build this together."
- **Listen:** "Okay, your turn to choose."
- **Feel their impact:** "He cried when I took the toy. I can fix that."

These micro-moments teach empathy and moral reasoning. In disagreements, children practice conflict resolution, a vital skill that no lecture could ever teach as effectively.

For emotionally complex children, peer play can be both healing and challenging. Some may prefer structure or smaller groups. They might struggle with rejection or overstimulation. Because of these challenges, supporting them as their caregiver might mean helping them find "just-right" playmates, children who share their rhythm, imagination, or sense of humor.

The Triangle Trouble Zone

When it comes to peer play, be thoughtful about group dynamics. Kids often thrive in one-on-one playdates or in slightly larger groups. What's most challenging is the classic "triangle" of three children together. It's the least stable social configuration, and it easily slips into two-against-one dynamics, even with kind, well-intentioned kids.

For emotionally complex or sensitive children, that extra social pressure can be overwhelming. They may end up feeling excluded or unintentionally become the one doing the excluding. Neither supports healthy social learning.

A simple guideline: when possible, choose pairs or small groups of four or more. It creates a safer, more balanced environment where everyone has room to connect and succeed.

Parent-Child Play: The Mirror of Worth

Playing with your child is not about entertainment; it's about *connection.* When you join their play world, you're telling them, *You matter so much that I want to see life through your eyes.*

This type of play boosts self-esteem and a sense of belonging. You give your child the most valuable resource you have: your time.

Examples of this can include:

- You crawl on the floor to build a city of blocks together.
- You let them "cook" a pretend meal for you and you actually eat it with delight.
- You become the audience for their one-person puppet show.

In those moments, you're co-regulating through joy. Your tone, laughter, and presence all communicate emotional safety. This shared play tells a child's nervous system, *You are seen. You are enough.*

Play as Emotional Language

Emotions are the characters that live inside play. Watch closely, and you'll see the full emotional spectrum unfold: triumph when the tower stands, frustration when it falls, sadness when the game ends, and joy when laughter erupts again.

Play gives children a safe, symbolic space to feel *everything.*

A child may rescue dolls from a fire or a loud flushing toilet *(processing fear).*

Another may line up animals after an argument at school *(restoring order to an inner chaos).*

Through play, emotions become tangible, manageable, and meaningful.

Play as Language Development

Language grows in motion, not in stillness. As children play, they narrate their world, assign roles, describe plans, and negotiate meaning. Every phrase they invent ("You can't go there unless you're wearing your magic cape!") is an exercise in cognitive flexibility and imagination.

Play fuels the parts of the brain responsible for both communication and executive functioning, the very abilities that emotionally complex kids often struggle with.

When a child says, "No, not like that, this way," they might simply be asserting independence and developing a sense of control. But for a neurodiverse child, that "no" can reflect a deeper need for order, logic, or sameness, because their nervous system finds comfort and safety in routines that make sense to them.

When they describe a made-up character's emotions, they're projecting dormant parts of themselves, while also rehearsing empathy and perspective taking.

Play is the bridge between thought and language, the birthplace of emotional literacy.

Play as Healing

Play gives order to disorder. Research in child development and play therapy consistently shows that play allows children to heal trauma, anxiety, and confusion. It gives their subconscious a stage to express what words cannot.

Through stories, art, building, and pretend scenarios, children externalize what's too big to hold inside. A child whose parents are divorcing may play "two houses." A child recovering from a hospital stay may "heal" dolls with bandages.

As a parent, knowing this changes everything. It means your role isn't to correct or direct their play, but to witness and join when invited, to become a trusted character in their unfolding story.

The Unique Play of Emotionally Complex Kids

Emotionally complex children often play differently. Some prefer quiet, methodical play rather than dramatic pretend scenes. Others engage you simply by showing what they're doing, not by assigning roles.

Many of these kids naturally think like engineers and architects. Their play lives in the world of problem-solving, building, and spatial brilliance. When you lean in with admiration, asking about their ideas, noticing their choices, and appreciating their process, you're stepping directly into their play world. You don't need to match their mastery; your interest is what matters. For them, being seen and understood in their creative process *is* play.

Your job is to meet them where they are. Join gently, observe with curiosity, and follow their lead. Even if their play looks serious or repetitive, it's still communication. They might be showing mastery, exploring control, or simply inviting you into their focus.

Sometimes the play isn't emotional but *relational.* They just want to share space with you, doing something they're proud of. That *is* connection. When a child feels connection, they feel seen, valued, and worthwhile, and that, at its core, is what it means to understand the emotional system that lives in all of us.

Decode Message

When your child plays, they're not just passing time; they're revealing their inner world. Play is their language before words fully catch up.

Decoded: *"I'm trying to make sense of my feelings, my world, and myself. Come see it through my eyes."*

By valuing play, solo, peer, or with you, you give your child permission to express, explore, and regulate their emotions in the safest way possible.

 Connection Moment

Set aside 15 minutes today for follow-their-lead play. No teaching. No correcting. No multitasking. No phones.

Let your child direct the scene, whether that means lining up cars, drawing, or assigning you the role of the "dragon." Stay in the story. Mirror their joy, curiosity, or even frustration.

If your child prefers quiet play, simply sit nearby and observe out loud:

"I love watching how focused you are," or "You look so proud of what you built."

That moment of presence tells your child: *You and your world matter to me.*

And in that moment, play has done what it was always meant to do: build the bridge between heart, mind, and relationship.

Chapter Three

Emotion by Design: Modeling and Meaning

Every parent shapes the emotional climate of their home, whether they realize it or not. Our tone, our expressions, and even the silence between words create the emotional blueprint our children come to rely on. What we model becomes what they mirror. What we explain becomes what they understand.

This chapter is about how our way of *being* and our way of *making sense* become our child's emotional education.

Modeling: The Silent Teacher

Children don't learn emotional regulation from what we tell them; they learn it from how we live. They study us constantly, taking in our every sigh, reaction, and attempt at repair.

When we respond to stress with composure, we teach safety.

When we repair after a mistake, we teach accountability.

When we express emotion honestly but calmly, we teach permission and control in the same breath.

Modeling doesn't mean being perfect, but it does mean being real, reflective, and intentional.

For emotionally complex children, this is even more crucial. These kids are emotional mimics by design. They absorb tone and energy like sponges. If a parent's reactions are unpredictable, their nervous systems become watchtowers, always scanning for safety cues. But when parents model steadiness, children internalize that calm as something they can access, too.

Modeling is the steady heartbeat that tells the child, *You can feel big things and still be okay.*

Meaning: The Missing Ingredient in Motivation

Many parents wish their children would simply cooperate, follow instructions, do what's asked, and trust that adults know best. And in early childhood, that dynamic mostly works. Young kids naturally look to parents for guidance, and they comply out of closeness and dependence.

But as children grow, and especially for neurodiverse or emotionally complex kids, *meaning* becomes the motivator. If they don't understand the "why" behind something, it often feels arbitrary, confusing, or even disrespectful to their logic-driven minds.

When you explain the *reason* for a request, you're not giving up authority. Instead, you're grounding authority in understanding. Meaning helps their brain file your request into a coherent story. Without it, your message lands as noise, and they naturally shut down or resist.

A child who hears, "Because I said so," learns obedience without comprehension.

A child who hears, "We do it this way because it keeps things fair and safe," learns both structure and purpose.

Meaning gives them something to *align* with, not just something to *submit* to.

The Collaboration Shift

Children, especially those who think and feel deeply, thrive in relationships built on mutual respect. That doesn't mean equal power; it means equal humanity. When you treat your child as a thinking person who deserves to understand the reasoning behind your boundaries, you activate their natural problem-solving brain rather than their defensive one.

A collaborative parent might say: "I know this rule feels unfair; let's talk about why it matters," or "Here's what I'm trying to protect you from. What do you think would make this easier?"

These small shifts don't undermine authority; they create shared meaning. When children feel invited into understanding, they no longer feel controlled. They feel connected.

The Intersection of Modeling and Meaning

Meaning without modeling is just talk, and modeling without meaning can feel authoritarian. But when you bring them together, you give your child something rare: a lived example *and* a reason to follow it.

If you ask your child to calm down while you're yelling, your modeling cancels your message. But if you stay regulated, narrate your process, and explain the purpose behind calmness ("I'm slowing my voice so we can both think clearly") you are combining emotion with logic, safety with sense.

That combination teaches emotional literacy at its highest level.

Why Emotionally Complex Kids Need This the Most

For emotionally complex or neurodiverse children, meaning provides stability. Their brains crave patterns and predictability. Knowing *why* something happens helps organize a chaotic world.

These children often have strong internal logic and will challenge authority, not to rebel but to seek clarity. When we interpret that as disrespect, we miss their real message: "Help me understand how this makes sense."

When they can connect meaning to behavior, when they know *why* it matters, they are far more likely to engage, cooperate, and self-regulate.

Understanding the Chain Reaction

When meaning is missing, frustration rises. The child resists. The parent feels disrespected. Tempers flare. The parent models agitation, and the child mirrors it back, each triggering the other in a closed feedback loop.

But when meaning is present, the loop reverses.

Clarity breeds calm.

Understanding reduces fear.

And empathy replaces resistance.

This is how modeling and meaning work together to shape emotional development from the inside out.

Decode Message

Children aren't defying you when they ask *why*. They're asking for meaning, safety, and connection.

Decoded: *"I want to understand the reason behind your world, so I can feel safe in mine."*

Connection Moment

Try this simple practice:

The next time your child resists a direction, pause and explain your intent in one calm sentence.

"I'm not asking you to clean up because I'm mad; I'm asking because a clean space helps our brains rest."

Then, ask them what they think:

"Does that make sense to you?"

That simple exchange transforms compliance into understanding, and understanding is where cooperation begins.

Chapter Four

The Complexity of Behavior: Deciphering What Children Can't Put Into Words

We often see kids through the lens of their behavior. We see the tantrum, the door slam, the shutdown, the refusal, and naturally, we draw conclusions. But behavior is not the full story. Behavior is the *message*, not the *meaning*. It's the final clue in a long chain of experiences that started long before that moment.

When we slow down enough to wonder, *What lies beneath this behavior?* we begin to see the world the way our children do. We stop reacting and start interpreting. And that's where the magic happens: in the decoding.

For most children, behavior is only a symptom of an unmet need. With this in mind, we can start anticipating their struggles before they erupt. We can meet needs early instead of mopping up the aftermath. But that requires something we often rush past: curiosity, patience, and a genuine willingness to look underneath.

When Behavior Speaks Louder Than Words

Children are new to this world. They've had only a handful of years to learn what takes adults decades to master: self-awareness, language, emotional control, problem solving. So when they're overwhelmed, confused, or undernourished, they don't use words; they use *behavior.*

Some kids show their distress on the outside; they yell, throw, argue, or stomp away. Others pull inward; they get quiet, avoid eye contact, or say, "I don't care," when they actually care deeply. And some kids do both, depending on the situation or the audience.

For emotionally complex and neurodiverse children, behavior becomes their main translator. These children might have advanced vocabularies, but they have limited expressive abilities when under stress. Their words vanish just when they need them most. So what you see, the shouting, the tears, the retreat, is the body stepping in to communicate what words cannot.

That's why it's so important to ask: *What are they trying to say with this behavior?*

What Happens Right Before It Happens

Quite often, I hear from families that schools only report the *aftermath*, what happened *after* a child became dysregulated or non-cooperative. What's often missing is the *precursor*, the "what happened before" that triggered the response.

For emotionally complex kids, that moment of escalation is rarely random; it's the nervous system's signal of overwhelm. When educators and caregivers understand the lead-up, not just the fallout, we gain the power to prevent rather than react. With the right supports, insight, and staff awareness, we can guide these children toward identifying solutions and finding their way back to regulation, a critical step in their emotional development.

Children rarely misbehave "out of nowhere." If we can identify what occurred just before a behavior got big, we often find the answer. Maybe your child had to stop a preferred activity. Maybe a sound became too loud. Maybe they were hungry or worried about something you didn't even realize mattered.

Think of it like being a detective, not a disciplinarian.

For example, if your child throws a pencil the moment math homework begins, the real message might be, "This feels too hard, and I'm scared I'll fail."

If your child "forgets" their instrument every Tuesday, maybe it's not forgetfulness at all; maybe it's embarrassment from being called out by the music teacher last week.

Once you uncover what came before, the behavior starts to make sense.

Why Language Isn't Always the Problem, Until It Is

Language development and emotional regulation are tightly linked. Some kids can articulate beautifully when they're calm but lose all access to language when stressed. Others struggle with language even at baseline, so frustration builds much faster.

A neurodiverse or gifted child who has advanced vocabulary might *sound* like an adult but *feel* like a five-year-old when things go wrong. Their words give an illusion of control, but underneath, they might be flooded with confusion or fear.

And then there are children who can't get the words out at all, who freeze or stumble when they're put on the spot. The words exist in their mind, but anxiety or overload scrambles their access to them. That's when we see behaviors that look "odd," "random," or "defiant," when really, they're communication substitutes.

If we can remember that every child wants to be understood, even when they don't have the words, we become less reactive and more compassionate translators.

Regulation Starts in the Body with Food

Before we jump to discipline or consequence, we must ask one simple question: *Has my child eaten?*

It may sound too simple, but nutrition is the foundation of regulation. An underfed brain cannot communicate, problem solve, or behave reasonably. Blood sugar dips, the prefrontal cortex loses access to logic, and the body's stress response takes over.

So, when you see behavior flare up, start with the basics:

- Have they eaten?
- Are they thirsty?
- Have they moved their body today?

- Are they overstimulated, too bright, too loud, too much?

If the answer to any of those is yes, meet the body first. You can't reason with a hungry or overstimulated brain. Once the body calms, language and cooperation often return on their own.

Although snacks can hold a child over, they aren't true nourishment. Crackers and veggies don't give the brain what it needs to regulate. A warm meal with protein and healthy fats will always support emotional balance more effectively.

If your child takes stimulant medication, the "come-down" period isn't just the medicine wearing off; it's also the body signaling a drop in blood sugar and energy regulation. Without stable blood sugar and proper electrolytes, the brain struggles to stay balanced, making emotional regulation and clear thinking much harder. Supporting your child with nourishing food and hydration after medication is essential; it helps the nervous system recover and sustain the focus and calm their body has been working so hard to maintain.

The Need to Feel Heard

Another question to ask: *Does my child feel understood?*

When kids don't feel heard, cooperation evaporates. It's true for adults too: the moment we feel misunderstood, our defenses rise. For a child, especially one who's anxious or neurodiverse, feeling unheard is intolerable. Their anxiety skyrockets, and words become inaccessible.

In those moments, our best move isn't correction, it's

connection.

Try saying: "I can see that really upset you," or "I think you felt that wasn't fair, am I close?"

You don't have to agree with them; you just have to *get them.* Once they feel understood, the brain relaxes. The nervous system settles. And suddenly, there's space for problem solving again.

Becoming the Investigator Instead of the Judge

Decoding behavior takes practice. It means stepping back from what's loud or disruptive and asking, *What need is unspoken here?*

Maybe your child is melting down every morning, not because they're defiant, but because transitions are hard. Maybe bedtime battles aren't about defiance but about anxiety and separation.

Over time, you start to notice patterns, the times of day, the environments, or even the people, that help you predict certain behaviors. When you understand your child's patterns, you move from *reacting* to *anticipating.* That's the real power of emotional decoding.

If your child throws their backpack the minute they walk through the door, it's not random. It's a signal: *I've held it together all day, and I need space before I can re-engage.*

If your child melts down over a tiny change in dinner plans, the message might be: *Too many changes today. I need predictability or a place to rest my brain and body.*

When you start to think like an emotional detective, the mystery of behavior begins to dissolve.

What They Do vs. What They Mean

Let's take a few common behaviors and look underneath them:

- **Refusal to start a task:** The child may not know where or how to begin. Breaking the task into a single, concrete first step can lower anxiety.
- **Arguing every detail:** This often means they need control or clarity. When they understand the "why" or get a choice in "how," the conflict softens.
- **Silliness at the wrong time:** Humor can be a pressure valve. It may be their way of releasing tension or regaining control.
- **Sudden silence or freeze:** This isn't defiance; it's shutdown. They're overwhelmed and can't retrieve words. Give them time and alternate ways to express themselves.
- **Explosive "NO!" response:** They need time, predictability, and reassurance that they're safe.

Once you know what these moments mean, your response changes. You're no longer fighting behavior, but instead, you're partnering with the brain behind it.

Helping Kids Who Can't Find Their Words

Some children simply can't express what they feel when they're flooded. You can help by offering alternate forms of communication.

You might say, "Point to what you want," or "Show me how big it feels," or even, "Would you rather draw it?"

You can use feelings charts, a "how hard is this moment" chart, hand signals, or a 1–5 scale for overwhelm. Reducing the demand for verbal language helps your child show you the truth, not the performance.

The goal isn't to get them to talk faster but to give them a safe lane to be understood.

The Body–Brain–Behavior Chain

Every observable behavior starts in the body, then moves through the brain, and ends in action. If we interrupt that process earlier, by calming the body or clarifying the thought, we can prevent the behavior from exploding outward.

So, the next time you see a behavior, ask yourself these three questions in order:

1. **Is their body okay?** *Are they hungry, tired, or overstimulated?*
2. **Is their brain supported?** *Do they understand the demand, do they feel safe, and do they have tools?*
3. **Is their connection secure?** *Do they feel seen and understood?*

When we tend to those three layers, behavior naturally shifts, without force or punishment.

Decode Message

Every behavior is a clue, a story in motion. It's your child's nervous system saying, *Something isn't right, help me name it.*

Decoded: *"I can't tell you what I need yet. Please slow down, see me, and help me find the words."*

Connection Moment

The next time your child acts out, instead of asking, "Why are you doing this?" try saying:

"Something about this is hard for you. Let's figure it out together."

Pause, offer food or quiet, and wait. The pause itself communicates safety. When their body calms, you can begin exploring meaning.

Over time, this approach teaches your child a powerful truth: their behavior isn't shameful; it's meaningful. And you are someone who can help them translate it.

Chapter Five

Beyond Defiance: Understanding Limit-Testing as Cognitive and Moral Growth

I can't tell you how many times I've sat across from a parent in my office who, after months of frustration, looks up and says, "I think my child has Oppositional Defiant Disorder." It's almost always said with both relief and worry: relief that there might be a name for the chaos, and worry that it means something permanent.

But here's what I gently remind them: any child who's emotionally complex or neurodiverse, whether that's autism or ADHD, is going to show defiance at some point. It's not their diagnosis; it's a developmental stage, a communication pattern, and sometimes, a coping strategy.

Defiance, in most cases, should not be seen as a disorder. It's a *signal.*

What Defiance Really Means

The word "defiance" often conjures images of willful rebellion, a child glaring and saying, "No!" just to make us mad.

But true defiance is far more nuanced. It simply means *to resist or challenge authority or expectations.* And children resist for many reasons: confusion, fear, fatigue, overstimulation, or a deep need for control in a world that often controls them.

When we label a child "defiant," we tend to stop asking questions. But defiance always has a story.

Sometimes a child resists because they're tired of failing. Sometimes it's because they're overwhelmed and can't articulate why. And sometimes it's because they're asserting an emerging sense of self, testing their independence, integrity, or voice.

A child who refuses to start homework might not be lazy; they might just be avoiding the humiliation of feeling incapable, or they may lack organizational skills and therefore struggle with motivation.

A child who talks back might not be intentionally disrespectful; they might be trying to express fairness in the only language they know: intensity with impulsivity.

Defiance is rarely about wanting to make an adult angry. It's more often about wanting to be seen, heard, or understood.

The Lag Behind the "No"

Children who struggle with emotional regulation or executive functioning often have lagging skills in starting, persisting, or transitioning. When those areas lag behind their age expectations, defiance becomes their default defense.

If a child is emotionally behind but cognitively bright,

the mismatch can be exhausting. They *know* what to do; they just can't get themselves to do it. So when you say, "Clean your room," and they respond with, "No!" or "In a minute!" what they're really saying is, "I don't have the bandwidth to start right now."

Neurodiverse children may have rigid thought patterns that make shifting from one task to another feel disorienting. Their "no" is an anchor in a world that keeps pulling them forward too fast. It's not defiance for the sake of power; it's a nervous system saying, *I'm not ready yet.*

Limit-Testing: The Hidden Work of Growth

Now let's talk about limit-testing, the behavior that drives parents to the edge but secretly shows incredible progress.

Limit-testing is not about defying authority but about exploring possibility. When a child asks, "Why can't I?" or "What if I do it this way instead?" they're flexing critical thinking muscles. They're learning about negotiation, power, and independence.

Children don't yet carry adult responsibilities, so their minds are freer to test out "what ifs." The same curiosity that makes them ask endless questions in preschool is what makes them challenge boundaries later. They're experimenting with *how far their influence reaches.*

This can look like:

- Asking for "five more minutes" after you've already said no

- Bargaining for one more show, one more snack, or one more turn
- Questioning your reasoning, not out of disrespect, but out of logic and fairness

To a tired parent, it can feel relentless. But from a developmental lens, it's evidence of *cognitive expansion.*

They're learning where they end and others begin. They're exploring cause and effect, reasoning, persuasion, and emotional intelligence, even if they don't realize it.

Every negotiation is a mini-lesson in self-advocacy, problem solving, and moral understanding.

The Emerging Morality of the Growing Brain

Around ages ten to twelve, a fascinating shift begins to happen. Children start forming their own moral compass. Their sense of right and wrong becomes less about what Mom or Dad says and more about internal principles, fairness, justice, loyalty, truth.

This is the foundation of moral growth, and it can feel uncomfortable for parents because it often shows up as questioning or debate. A child who once accepted every rule now wants to know *why* the rule exists. They start comparing your decisions to what they see in friends' families or at school.

And while this can sound like arguing, it's really reasoning. Their brain is practicing empathy and moral differentiation. They're beginning to ask, "What kind of person do I want to be?"

Not only are children asking themselves who they want to become, but they've also been watching *you* for years, quietly discerning which parts of you feel familiar and which they need to leave behind to grow into themselves. This process, though often invisible, is the essence of becoming a whole and separate person. It can be hard to witness because it unfolds right in front of us, both physically and emotionally, as they differentiate from us in real time. It's a stage deserving of deep respect and quiet understanding, so that connection can remain strong through these turbulent years of becoming.

When parents meet this stage with curiosity instead of control, by listening, validating, and discussing values, they help shape that moral growth rather than shutting it down.

If a child says, "That's not fair," instead of answering, "Life's not fair," try saying, "Tell me what feels unfair to you." You might discover a remarkable sense of logic and integrity behind the pushback.

Defiance as Dialogue

If we reframe defiance as communication rather than rebellion, we stop taking it personally. The "no" becomes an invitation to slow down and investigate the meaning behind the action.

It's hard not to take it personally when your child comes at you with anger, harsh words, or defiance. In those moments, it can feel deeply hurtful. But remember: your child isn't trying to make you feel like a bad parent or a bad person.

They're struggling to be seen, understood, and accepted unconditionally.

As adults, we have more life experience and perspective, which means we can pause and look beyond the surface behavior. When we take things personally, we lose sight of context, of where our child's lagging skills, sensitivities, or disabilities might be driving their reactions. It's not about you being a "bad parent." It's about understanding where your child needs more support and compassion.

When we stop personalizing their behavior, we open the door to connection. We begin to see our children as whole humans, doing the best they can with the tools they have, and that shift is where real growth, for both parent and child, begins.

Ask yourself:

- What is my child trying to express?
- What need might not be met?
- What skill might be lagging?
- What belief are they trying to test?

When we stay calm enough to ask these questions, we shift from power struggles to problem solving. And this shift changes everything, because children who feel understood are far more likely to cooperate.

When Morals and Boundaries Collide

A child developing their moral compass may call out inconsistencies. They'll say things like, "But you said not to yell, and now you're yelling!" or "You told me honesty matters, but you lied about the dentist appointment."

It can sting, but it's a sign of moral growth. They're holding up a mirror, one that shows how deeply they're paying attention to *meaning.*

Your best response isn't to defend yourself but to model humility. "You're right, I did say that. I should've handled it differently." That kind of honesty builds more respect than authority ever will.

Moral development doesn't end in childhood. It evolves through conversations, corrections, and connection. And when your child trusts that their thoughts and values are respected, your influence lasts far longer than any rule ever could.

Seeing the Big Picture

Defiance, limit-testing, and moral growth are not separate chapters of development; they're interconnected steps on the path to autonomy. The child who questions, negotiates, and stands their ground is the same child who will later know how to advocate for themselves, protect their boundaries, and think critically about the world.

As parents, we may long for compliance, but what our children need is *competence.* They need to know how to think, not just obey. And sometimes, that learning process looks messy.

So the next time your child challenges you, see it as a sign of cognitive expansion. The next time they refuse, see it as emotional data. The next time they argue a rule, see it as a budding moral compass at work.

Defiance is not the enemy of development. It's the training ground for independence.

Decode Message

Defiance is communication in disguise.

Decoded: *"I'm trying to figure out where my power begins and ends. Please stay calm and help me understand the boundaries without taking away my voice."*

Connection Moment

When your child says "no" or challenges a rule, take one breath before you respond. Instead of tightening control, turn curiosity on.

Try saying: "You sound like you feel strongly about this. Tell me what's important to you right now."

Listen without rushing to correct. Then, calmly restate your boundary and your reason: "I hear what you're saying. Here's why this boundary matters, and here's where I can give you some choice."

That one moment of understanding shows your child that boundaries and respect can coexist, and that their growing independence doesn't have to threaten your connection.

Chapter Six

When the Brain Fights Back: Supporting Kids Before Dysregulated Meltdowns

When I meet with families in my practice, I often hear parents describe their child's difficult moments as "meltdowns" or "tantrums." Those words aren't wrong, but they don't tell the whole story. Instead, I like to call it what it truly is: dysregulation.

When we use the term *dysregulation,* it helps everyone, child and parent, understand that this isn't bad behavior or a lack of discipline. It's a nervous system in distress. It's the brain and body saying, *I'm overwhelmed, and I can't hold it together right now.*

What Dysregulation Really Means

Dysregulation simply means that a child can't organize their thoughts and feelings at the same time. The two systems, thinking and feeling, lose connection. The emotional brain (the limbic system) takes over, while the rational brain (the prefrontal cortex) goes offline.

When that happens, emotions become incoherent. They're too big, too fast, too confusing for the child to manage. So those emotions spill out through behavior, yelling, crying, running away, freezing, or collapsing in frustration.

In other words, dysregulated emotions lead to dysregulated behavior. And once the behavior takes over, the child no longer has access to the part of the brain that helps them make good choices or communicate clearly. That's why it's so important to catch dysregulation *before* it spirals. The earlier we step in, the easier it is for our child to come back to balance.

The Power of Prediction and Prevention

One of the most valuable skills a parent can develop is the ability to anticipate dysregulation. The more you understand your child's nervous system, the easier it becomes to see the signs before the storm hits.

Children rarely go from calm to chaos without clues. Maybe their voice tightens. Maybe their shoulders rise or they stomp their feet. Maybe they start using short, clipped answers or avoiding eye contact. Maybe they start pacing, grunting, making exasperated sounds, or asking repetitive questions. These are early indicators that the brain is starting to lose coherence.

For example, imagine your child has just come home from school. They throw their water bottle on the counter and snap when you ask how their day went. That's your cue. Instead of matching their energy or demanding respect, pause. You might say, "Looks like it was a long day. Do you want to eat something first or have a little quiet time before we talk?"

By seeing the moment before the meltdown, you've prevented the meltdown altogether. You've caught the nervous system before it fell off the cliff.

It's also worth noting that our own timing and expectations can sometimes be the trigger. If we're focused on our agenda, homework, dinner prep, schedules, right as our child walks through the door, we may unintentionally ignite dysregulation. Their nervous system is coming off hours of effort, structure, and sensory demand. Jumping straight into "what's next" can feel like too much, too soon.

A wise parent learns to read the room, or rather, the child. Put your child's immediate needs first when they come home: nourishment, decompression, reconnection. The routine can wait a few minutes. Those few minutes of empathy often prevent an evening of reactivity.

When a child feels seen and prioritized, their nervous system relaxes, and cooperation naturally follows.

When We Miss the Signs

If we miss those early warning signals, the child's nervous system goes into full protection mode, the body's built-in alarm system known as *fight, flight, or freeze.*

Once that alarm sounds, the logical brain is offline. The child is not *choosing* their reaction; their nervous system is. It's not a character flaw, and it's not disrespect. It's biology.

A *fight* response might look like yelling, hitting, or arguing.

A *flight* response might look like running away, hiding, or trying to escape a demand.

A *freeze* response might look like total shutdown, blank stare, no words, disconnection.

Each of these is a form of protection. The brain perceives a threat, not necessarily a physical one, but an emotional one. It could be fear of failure, embarrassment, pressure, or even sensory overload.

When the brain feels threatened, cortisol surges and floods the system. The heart races, breathing quickens, muscles tighten. At that point, no amount of reasoning or consequence will work. The nervous system must first return to safety.

The Recovery Window

Here's what many parents don't realize: once a child becomes fully dysregulated, it can take *hours* for their body to return to a calm baseline. Even if they seem fine after ten minutes, their nervous system is still on high alert underneath.

You may have had this experience: after an evening of dysregulation, you check on your child and find them sleeping, their small body still hiccupping between breaths. Those quiet tremors are the nervous system's way of releasing tension and finding calm. Regulation doesn't happen instantly; it takes time for a child's body to return to balance, even while they sleep. It's a reminder of just how hard their nervous system works to find safety again, and how much grace they need during the process.

That's why prevention is key. The goal isn't to avoid emotion altogether, that's impossible. The goal is to catch emotional overload *before* it turns into full dysregulation.

When you learn your child's patterns, when they're hungry, tired, overstimulated, or anxious, you can step in early. A calm tone, a snack, a brief pause, or even simple acknowledgment can change everything.

Learning to See the World Through Their Eyes

Children live in a sensory-rich world that feels bigger than ours. They notice textures, sounds, and social nuances that we may miss entirely. A crowded classroom, a loud sibling or car, or even a bright light can send their nervous system into overload without them knowing why.

Therefore, the best gift you can give your child is your perspective. Step into their shoes. Notice what environments make them calm versus what overstimulates them. When you start to see the world through their eyes, you'll begin to anticipate what's too much and what helps restore balance.

Let's say you're headed to a family gathering, and your child tends to get overwhelmed in social settings. Instead of hoping for the best, *plan for the nervous system*. Prepare your child for what to expect and for how long. Bring noise-canceling headphones. Keep snacks and fun puzzles or activities handy. Inform your family so they can support you and your child.

That's not coddling. It's preparing their brain for success.

Teaching in the Moment, Not Punishing After

Once a child has gone over the edge into a full meltdown, teaching is impossible. Their brain isn't in a state that can absorb logic or lessons. At that point, your only job is safety and calm presence.

Then, once your child's nervous system has calmed and they're able to listen and think clearly, that's the moment when true learning can happen. In that window of calm, their brain is open, connected, and ready to absorb your guidance. If we wait too long, an hour or until the next day, the opportunity for growth is often lost.

But shortly after safety and connection have been restored, once they've had food, rest, or quiet, understanding naturally follows. That's when gentle teaching can take root. You can gently reflect: "That got really big earlier. What felt the hardest for you?" Or: "I noticed your body was really tense before you got upset. Next time, maybe that can be our clue to take a break earlier."

When handled this way, each episode becomes a teaching moment instead of a shame spiral. You're not punishing emotion but training awareness.

Dysregulation vs. Manipulation: Understanding the Difference

When a child is dysregulated, their nervous system has lost its sense of safety, and ignoring true dysregulation often deepens the distress and makes recovery harder.

A *manipulative tantrum*, on the other hand, has a different energy. It's more about testing limits or trying to influence an outcome, like stomping feet, protesting boundaries, or negotiating for what they want. These moments still require empathy, but they also call for gentle structure and consistency.

Both experiences are opportunities for connection: one invites soothing, the other requires steady guidance. The more we learn to tell them apart, the better we can support our children in building emotional awareness and trust.

When a child is dysregulated, they're not being manipulative. They're not trying to "get their way." They're trying to get back to *okay*.

Dysregulation is a nervous system event. And nervous systems need time, attunement, and co-regulation, not punishment, to recover. When we meet dysregulation with empathy and consistency, the brain learns that safety can exist even in strong emotion. That's how resilience is built.

Helping the Brain Before It Fights Back

When we understand that fight, flight, and freeze are protective responses, we can intervene compassionately.

If your child goes into fight, don't meet fire with fire. Lower your tone. Use fewer words. Soften your body language. They're looking for your nervous system to borrow calm from.

If they flee, give them permission to step away. Say, "I can see you need space. I'll be here when you're ready." That signals safety, not abandonment. When a child runs away, it's often not defiance; it's fear. Many children who elope are scared they're in trouble or uncertain about how the adult will respond. Their nervous system is signaling danger, even when none exists. Sometimes, the simplest reassurance, softly saying, "You're not in trouble, you're safe," can have a powerful calming effect. What they need most in that moment is clear direction, emotional safety, and your steady presence. That's how trust begins to replace fear.

If they freeze, speak gently and move slowly. Offer presence without demand. "It's okay. I'm right here. Take your time."

Each of these moments is a lesson in emotional regulation. You're teaching coping skills in real time, not by *talking* about calm, but by *being* calm.

Meltdowns as Missed Opportunities

When meltdowns happen frequently, it's not proof that your child is broken or that you've failed. It's simply data. It tells us there's a gap between what the child can handle and what they're currently being asked to do.

A meltdown is a message: *I've reached my limit.*

Our job isn't to make that message go away but to learn from it.

When we take note of when, where, and why dysregulation happens, we become better predictors. And when we predict, we can prevent.

Decode Message

A meltdown is never random. It's your child's nervous system crying out for help before words can form.

Decoded: *"My brain feels unsafe, and I don't know how to fix it. Please help me slow down before it gets too big."*

Connection Moment

Choose one daily scenario that tends to push your child to the edge, mornings, homework, transitions, bedtime. Before it begins, quietly say to yourself, "I'm the regulator."

Then watch for early signs: a clenched jaw, fidgeting, tone changes, avoidance. Step in gently, not with demands, but with support: "Looks like this part feels hard. Let's pause for a snack, a stretch, or a breath before we start again."

That tiny, preventative action teaches your child that emotions don't have to explode to be noticed; they can be understood, contained, and soothed.

When we become the calm before the storm, our children's brains learn that safety can exist even in chaos. And that's when the brain stops fighting back, and starts trusting.

Chapter Seven

When Kids Resist: The Hidden Anxiety Behind Demand Avoidance

Demand avoidance" describes what happens when a child resists everyday requests, expectations, or instructions, often in ways that seem puzzling or defiant. For many neurodiverse kids, however, this isn't misbehavior; it's a *coping mechanism*. Their nervous system interprets even simple demands as pressure, triggering anxiety or a sense of losing control. Avoidance becomes their way of protecting themselves when the world feels too demanding or unpredictable.

Emotionally complex kids often have rich verbal skills, sharp reasoning, and boundless creativity. Yet when their emotions rise, those strengths can slip away, and they need an adult's steady presence to help them find calm again. It's easy to feel frustrated when your child resists your guidance, especially when the request seems small. But resistance isn't about willfulness; it's often about anxiety. Their still-developing emotional system struggles to tolerate the intensity of expectations, so even gentle directions can feel heavy.

Imagine how many times a day your child hears, "Stop," "Wait," "Don't," "Calm down." To a sensitive nervous system, these constant corrections can feel like a storm. So when another request arrives, even a simple one like, "Please grab your shoes," or "Let's get ready for bed," the instinctive response may be *no.*

One of the most effective ways to reduce resistance is to use *declarative language.*

Declarative language communicates through observation and curiosity instead of direct instruction. It's like walking through the back door rather than knocking on the front. Instead of saying, "Go get your backpack," you might try, "I notice your backpack's still by the door," or "I wonder if we're ready to go." The goal isn't to remove structure but to lighten it. Offering help ("Let's do it together") also eases the burden and communicates shared responsibility rather than pressure.

Another useful approach is creating an *equalizing moment.* Emotionally complex kids often feel that life is unfair, that everyone else gets the easier deal. Equalizing means coming to their level, acknowledging their perspective, and inviting input within your boundaries. When your child feels heard and respected, cooperation becomes possible. The more autonomy they experience in small, safe ways, the less they need to fight for control.

Demand avoidance can't be "cured," because it's not an illness; it's a coping pattern. But with awareness, we can learn to recognize when it shows up, reduce triggers, and guide children toward self-understanding and self-trust.

Understanding the Influence of Nonverbal Communication

Lastly, remember that nonverbal communication often speaks louder than words. Emotionally sensitive children are experts at reading faces, tone, and body language. If your words say, "I'm fine," but your body is tense or your expression rigid, your child feels the mismatch immediately. They're not being difficult; they're attuned to your energy. Their nervous system depends on congruence; when your tone, words, and body align, they feel safe.

Have you ever heard your child ask, "Are you mad at me?" and keep seeking reassurance? They're not being needy; they're reading your energy. Kids are incredibly perceptive. They can sense when something in you doesn't match your words, which can feel confusing and even a little scary. Their world suddenly feels uncertain.

If you're struggling to regulate in that moment, honesty is the most healing thing you can offer. You might say, "I'm feeling upset right now, and I need a few minutes to calm down. We'll be okay." That simple truth helps your child feel safe again. It teaches them that emotions are normal, that adults also need to regroup, and that calm can always return.

Emotionally complex kids don't just listen to what you say; they *feel* who you are. When your calm is authentic, they can finally let theirs emerge too.

Decode Message

Resistance is often the body's way of saying, *I'm overwhelmed.* What looks like defiance is frequently anxiety in disguise. These moments aren't about control or disrespect; they're a reflection of your child's nervous system trying to stay safe.

Decoded: *"Constant demands and corrections make me feel anxious and like I'm always doing something wrong. Please be patient with me as I'm learning to regulate my emotions."*

Connection Moment

Soften your tone, slow your pace, and shift from command to collaboration.

Try saying:

- "I notice you're not ready yet."
- "I wonder what feels hard about this."
- "Let's figure this out together."

If you sense frustration, pause and equalize the moment. Sit beside your child and acknowledge their experience: "I get why

that feels big." When your energy and body language match your calm words, your child senses safety, and from that place, connection can grow.

Chapter Eight

Co-Regulation: Growing Alongside Your Child

By now, you've learned more about your child's unique genetic makeup, their unfolding personality, their emotional regulation system, and your evolving role as their steady support and guide. As both of you move through new stages of growth, the work of regulation never truly ends; it simply transforms.

Every developmental chapter brings fresh challenges and opportunities for emotional growth. As your child matures, so will you. Parenting is a relationship between two developing humans, not a one-way teaching process. You grow together, adjusting, learning, and strengthening your bond through every stage. Over time, you'll find that your child becomes one of your greatest teachers, the mirror through which you learn patience, flexibility, and grace.

Dr. Stuart Shanker, in his work book *Self-Reg,* reminds us that the heart of nurturing emotional development lies in two-way communication. Even during the hardest moments, when frustration or disconnection threaten to pull you apart, your shared *inter-brain* connection allows you to stay attuned to one another. These moments of co-regulation are where emotional learning deepens. They're where courage, determination, hope, and compassion take root.

As Dr. Shanker also reminds us, it's natural for children to explore a wide range of emotions, not just the ones that feel exciting or joyful, but also those that feel frightening, disappointing, or uncertain. Our job isn't to protect them from those feelings, but to *walk beside them* through them. When we stay calm, engaged, and supportive, we offer the one thing every child needs most: safety amid chaos.

Your child may soon be ready for sports teams, classrooms, or debate clubs, but the greatest gift you can give them isn't academic or athletic. It's the ability to manage emotions, solve problems, and regulate impulses. These are the lifelong skills that build resilience and shape healthy relationships.

The Calm Connection That Lasts Forever

Even though your child has learned so many valuable lessons, through therapy, social groups, ABA, or simply under your steady, loving guidance, they will always need your presence by their side. Emotional maturity isn't something that happens all at once; an immature nervous system takes time to evolve, and that evolution never truly stops. The nature of your relationship will continue to grow and change as both of you do.

As your child moves through adolescence into early adulthood, your co-regulation skills will be as essential as ever. These moments of calm connection, where you breathe together through frustration, listen with empathy, and remind each other of safety, are the threads that will keep your bond strong for life.

There's no finish line to becoming a more evolved, emotionally attuned human. We're all learning to understand ourselves, layer by layer, with more insight and compassion. Every stage of your child's growth invites you to grow too. That is the quiet magic of parenting an emotionally complex child: it becomes a shared lifelong practice of understanding, patience, and love.

The ADHD or Naturally Intense Parent

All of this probably sounds meaningful and inspiring, but what if you recognize some of these traits in yourself? What if you have ADHD, or you're naturally intense, driven, and prone to anxious or rigid thinking? If so, this work may feel harder for you than for most, and that's okay. It makes perfect sense. DNA and biology shape all of us, and if you've passed along some of these traits to your child, it simply means you share a similar wiring. You're walking this path *together*.

Learning to regulate when your own nervous system runs fast, hypervigilant, or emotionally charged takes patience and support. That's why reaching out for help, through DBT, IFS therapy, coaching, or self-paced learning, isn't a sign of weakness; it's an act of wisdom. The more you understand and care for your own intensity, the more peace and predictability you can offer your child.

You are capable of doing this work. Your awareness is

already the first step. Regulation doesn't mean changing who you are but learning how to slow the current of your beautiful, powerful mind so both you and your child can move through life with more calm, connection, and joy.

Decode Message

Learning to stay balanced and connected is a practice that evolves with us through every age and season. Your child's nervous system learns regulation by borrowing yours. As you stay calm, present, and engaged, you teach them how to manage emotions, repair after conflict, and return to balance.

Co-regulation isn't just something we do *for* children; it's something we do *with* them. Through this ongoing exchange, both of you keep growing, together.

Decoded: *"I'm still learning about myself, and so are you! Let's be patient with each other and learn about ourselves together."*

Connection Moment

Pause and reflect on how far you've come. Every meltdown you've softened, every repair you've made, and every time you've chosen connection over control has shaped your child's emotional foundation.

Tonight, take a quiet moment to tell your child, "I love how we're learning together." Because you are, and that shared growth is the lifelong work of regulation.

In every storm that your child learns how to stand back up, it's your steady presence that teaches them where peace begins.

Closing Note

Dear parent,

If you've reached this page, you've already taken meaningful steps toward understanding your child more deeply. That effort matters. It creates steadier days, clearer connection, and a home that feels safer for everyone.

My hope is that these chapters offered you insight and a sense of relief, that things make a little more sense now, and that you feel more equipped than when you began. You're not alone in this. With the right support, even the hard moments become more manageable, and the small successes become easier to see.

If you want more individualized guidance, you can join me at TheMisunderstoodChild.com for personal family coaching and online parenting classes. It's simply another way for us to continue the work you've started here.

You've done something important. Keep going. You and your child deserve what comes next.

Sincerely,
Kimberley Clayton Blaine

For personal parent coaching or to enroll in the author's online seminars visit *TheMisunderstoodChild.com*

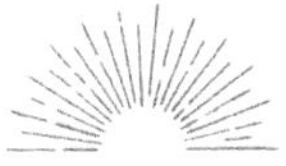

References

Aldort, N. (2006). *Raising our children, raising ourselves: Transforming parent-child relationships from reaction and struggle to freedom, power and joy*. Bothell, WA: Naomi Aldort, PhD (Book Publishers)

Barkley, R. A. (2022). *Treating ADHD in Children and Adolescents*. The Guilford Press.

Cohen, L. J. (2002). *Playful parenting*. New York: Ballantine Books.

Coronato, H. (2008). *Eco-friendly families: Guide your family to greener living with activities that engage and inspire* . . . from toddlers to teens. New York: Alpha.

Dombro, A., & Lerner, C. (2005). *Bringing up baby: Three steps to making good decisions in your child's first years*. Washington, DC: Zero to Three.

Dreikurs, R., & Soltz, V. (1980). *Children: The challenge: New York: Plume.*

Dundon, R. (2021). *PDA in the Therapy Room: A Clinician's Guide to Working with Children with Pathological Demand Avoidance*. Jessica Kingsley Publishers.

Dutwin, D. (2008). *Unplug your kids: A parent's guide to raising happy, active, and well-adjusted children in the digital age*. Cincinnati, OH: Adams Media.

Faber, A., & Mazlish, E. (1995). *How to talk so kids will listen and listen so kids will talk*. New York: Harper Paperbacks.

Garbarino, J., & Bedard, C. (2001). *Parents under siege: Why you are the solution, not the problem, in your child's life*. New York: Free Press.

Gavigan, C. (2008). *Healthy child healthy world*. New York: Dutton.

Ginott, H., & Ginott, A. (2003). *Between parent and child: The best-selling classic that revolutionized parent-child communication (Rev.* ed.). New York: Three Rivers Press.

Gottman, J. (1998). *Raising an emotionally intelligent child: The heart of parenting*. New York: Simon & Schuster.

Gottman, J., & Gottman, J. S. (2003). *And baby makes three: The six-step plan for preserving marital intimacy and rekindling romance after baby arrives*. New York: Three Rivers Press.

Grille, R. (2005). *Parenting for a peaceful world*. New South Wales, Australia: Longueville Media.

Hart, S., & Hodson, V. K. (2006). *Respectful parents, respectful kids: 7 keys to turn family conflicts into cooperation*. Encinitas, CA: Puddledancer Press.

Heim, S., & Engel-Smothers, H. (2008). *Boosting your baby's brain power*. Scottsdale, AZ: Great Potential Press.

Hirsh-Pasek, K., & Golinkoff, R. M. (2003). *Einstein never used flash cards: How our children really learn and why they need to play more and memorize less*. Emmaus, PA:

Rodale Books.

Holinger, P. (2003). *What babies say before they can talk: The nine signals infants use to express their feelings*. New York: Fireside.

Holt, J. C. (1995). *How children learn*. New York: Da Capo Press.

Hunter, A., & Walker, J. (2007). *The Moms on Call guide to basic baby care: The first 6 months*. Grand Rapids, MI: Revell.

Hyman, I. (1997). *The case against spanking: How to discipline your child without hitting*. San Francisco: JosseyBass.

Kashtan, I. (2005). *Parenting from your heart: Sharing the gifts of compassion, connection and choice*. Encinitas, CA: Puddledancer Press.

Kohn, A. (2005). *Unconditional parenting: Moving from rewards and punishments to love and reason*. New York: Atria.

Kurcinka, M. S. (2001). *Kids, parents and power struggles*. New York: Harper Paperbacks.

Kurcinka, M. S. (2007). *Sleepless in America: Is your child misbehaving or missing sleep? New York: Harper Paperbacks.*

Kvols, K. J. (1998). *Redirecting children's behavior*. Seattle: Parenting Press.

Lieberman, A. F. (1995). *The emotional life of the toddler*. New York: Free Press.

Markman, H., Stanley, S., & Blumberg, S. (2001). *Fighting for your marriage: Positive steps for preventing divorce and preserving divorce and preserving a lasting love*. San Francisco: Jossey-Bass.

Melmed, M. (1997, July). "Parents speak: Zero to Three's findings from research on parents' views of early childhood development. Public policy report." Young Children, 52(5), 46–49.

Miller, A. (2002). *For your own good: Hidden cruelty in child-rearing and the roots of violence (3rd ed.)*. New York: Farrar, Straus and Giroux.

Monteiro, Marilyn, J. (2016) *Family Therapy and Autism Spectrum*.

Murphy, Linda (2020) *Declarative Language Handbook*.

Perry, B. D. (1994). "Neurobiological sequelae of childhood trauma: Post traumatic stress disorders in children." In M. Murburg (Ed.), Catecholamine function in post traumatic stress disorder: Emerging concepts (pp. 253–276). Washington, DC: American Psychiatric Press.

Riak, J. (2009). *Plain talk about spanking*. Parents and Teachers Against Violence in Education.

Rosenberg, M. (2003). *Nonviolent communication: A language of life (2nd ed.)*. Encinitas, CA: Puddledancer Press.

Runkel, H. E. (2008). *Screamfree parenting: The revolutionary approach to raising your kids by keeping your cool*. New York: Broadway Books.

Schickedanz, J. (1999). *Much more than the ABCs: The early stages of reading and writing*. Washington, DC: National Association for the Education of Young Children.

Shanker, S. (2016). *Self-Reg: How to Help Your Child (and You) Break the Stress Cycle and Successfully Engage with Life*. Penguin Books.

Siegel, D., & Hartzell, M. (2001). *Parenting from the inside out: How a deeper understanding can help you raise children who thrive*. New York: Tarcher.

Sobel, D. (1999). *Beyond ecophobia: Reclaiming the heart in nature education*. Great Barrington, MA: Orion Society.

Straus, M. A. (1999, October 5). "Is it time to ban corporal punishment of children?" Journal of the Canadian Medical Association, 161, 821.

Swallow, W. K. (2000). *The shy child: Helping children triumph over shyness*. New York: Grand Central Publishing.

Teicher, M. H. (2002, March). "Scars that won't heal: The neurobiology of child abuse." Scientific American, 286(3), 68–75.

Wesselman, D. (1998). *The whole parent: How to become a terrific parent even if you didn't have one*. New York: Da Capo Press. 194

Best Book Corner

Books for Parents

Aldort, N., *Raising Our Children, Raising Ourselves: Transforming Parent-Child Relationships from Reaction and Struggle to Freedom, Power and Joy* (2006)

Cohen, L. J., *Playful Parenting* (2002)

Coronato, H., *Eco-Friendly Families: Guide Your Family to Greener Living with Activities That Engage and Inspire* .

. . *from Toddlers to Teens* (2008)
Dreikurs, R., and Soltz, V., *Children: the Challenge* (1980)
Dutwin, D., *Unplug Your Kids: A Parent's Guide to Raising Happy, Active, and Well-Adjusted Children in the Digital Age* (2008)
Faber, A., and Mazlish, E., *How to Talk So Kids Will Listen and Listen So Kids Will Talk* (1995)
Garbarino, J., *and Bedard, C. Parents Under Siege: Why You Are the Solution, Not the Problem, in Your Child's Life* (2001)
Ginott, H. G., *Between Parent and Child: The Bestselling Classic That Revolutionized Parent-Child Communication* (2003)
Gottman, J., *Raising an Emotionally Intelligent Child: The Heart of Parenting* (1998)
Gottman, J., and Gottman, J. S., *And Baby Makes Three* (2007)
Gottman, J., and Silver, N., *The Seven Principles for Making Marriage Work* (1999)
Greene, R. *Raising Human Beings: Creating a Collaborative Partnership with Your Child* (2016)

Children's book lists courtesy of the Center on the Social and Emotional Foundations for Early Learning (CSEFEL)

Gurian, M., *The Purpose of Boys: Helping Our Sons Find Meaning, Significance, and Direction in Their Lives* (2009)
Hart, S., and Hodson, V. K., *Respectful Parents, Respectful*

Kids: 7 Keys to Turn Family Conflicts into Cooperation (2006)

Heim, S., and Engel-Smothers, H., *Boosting Your Baby's Brain Power* (2008)

Hirsh-Pasek, K., and Golinkoff, R. M., *Einstein Never Used Flash Cards: How Our Children Really Learn and Why They Need to Play More and Memorize Less* (2003)

Holinger, P., *What Babies Say Before They Can Talk: The Nine Signals Infants Use to Express Their Feelings* (2003)

Holt, J. C., *How Children Learn* (1995)

Kashtan, I., *Parenting from Your Heart: Sharing the Gifts of Compassion, Connection, and Choice* (2004)

Kohn, A., *Unconditional Parenting: Moving from Rewards and Punishments to Love and Reason* (2005)

Kurcinka, M. S., *Kids, Parents, and Power Struggles* (2001)

Kurcinka, M. S., *Sleepless in America: Is Your Child Misbehaving . . . or Missing Sleep?* (2007)

Kvols, K. J., *Redirecting Children's Behavior* (1998)

Lerner, C., and Dombro, A. L., *Bringing Up Baby: Three Steps to Making Good Decisions in Your Child's First Years* (2005)

Markman, H., Stanley, S., and Blumberg, S., *Fighting for Your Marriage: Positive Steps for Preventing Divorce and Preserving a Lasting Love* (2001)

Pieper, M. H., and Pieper, W. J., *Smart Love: The Compassionate Alternative to Discipline That Will Make You a Better Parent and Your Child a Better Person* (1999)

Pipher, M., *Reviving Ophelia: Saving the Selves of Adolescent Girls* (1995)

Rosenberg, M. B., *Nonviolent Communication* (2003)

Runkel, H. E., *Screamfree Parenting: The Revolutionary Approach to Raising Your Kids by Keeping Your Cool* (2008)

Schickedanz, J. A., *Much More Than the ABCs: The Early Stages of Reading and Writing* (1999)

Siegel, D., and Hartzell, M., *Parenting from the Inside Out: How a Deeper Understanding Can Help You Raise Children Who Thrive* (2001)

Sobel, D., *Beyond Ecophobia: Reclaiming the Heart in Nature Education* (1996)

Swallow, W. K., *The Shy Child: Helping Children Triumph over Shyness* (2000)

Wesselman, D., *The Whole Parent: How to Become a Terrific Parent Even If You Didn't Have One* (1998)

Kid Books About Feelings

ABC Look at Me! by Roberta Grobel Intrater (infant–4)

Baby Faces books (most are by Roberta Grobel Intrater) (infant–4)

Big Feelings: A Book Filled with Emotions, Talaris Institute (2009)

Can You Tell How Someone Feels? by Nita Everly (3–6)

Double-Dip Feelings, by Barbara S. Cain (5–8)

The Feelings Book, by Todd Parr (3–8)

Glad Monster, Sad Monster, by Ed Emberley and Anne Miranda (infant–5)

The Grouchy Ladybug, by Eric Carle (1–6)
Happy and Sad, Grouchy and Glad, by Constance Allen (4–7)
How Are You Peeling: Foods with Moods/Vegetal Como Eres: Alimentos con Sentimientos, by Saxton Freymann (5–8)
How Do I Feel? by Norma Simon (2–7)
How Do I Feel?/Como Me Siento? ed. by the editors of the American Heritage Dictionaries (infant–4)
I Am Happy, by Steve Light (3–6)
If You're Happy and You Know It! by Jane Cabrera (3–6)
Little Teddy Bear's Happy Face, Sad Face, by Lynn Offerman (a first book about feelings)
Lizzy's Ups and Downs, by Jessica Harper (3–9)
My Many Colored Days, by Dr. Seuss (3–8)
On Monday When It Rained, by Cherryl Kachenmeister (3–8)
Proud of Our Feelings, by Lindsay Leghorn (4–8)
See How I Feel, by Julie Aigner-Clark (infant–4)
Sometimes I Feel Like a Storm Cloud, by Lezlie Evans (4–8)
Today I Feel Silly and Other Moods That Make My Day, by Jamie Lee Curtis (3–8)
The Way I Feel, by Janan Cain (3–8)
What I Look Like When I Am Confused/Como Me Veo Cuando Estoy Confundido, by Joanne Randolph (5–8)
What Makes Me Happy? by Catherine and Laurence Anholt (3–6)

Kid Books on Sad Feelings

Franklin's Bad Day, by Paulette Bourgeois and Brenda Clark (5–8)

Hurty Feelings, by Helen Lester (5–8)
Knuffle Bunny, by Mo Willems (3–6)
Let's Talk About Feeling Sad, by Joy Wilt Berry (3–5)
Smudge's Grumpy Day, by Miriam Moss (3–8)
Sometimes I Feel Awful, by Joan Singleton Prestine (5–8)
The Very Lonely Firefly, by Eric Carle (4–7)
When I Feel Sad, by Cornelia Maude Spelman (5–7)

Kid Books on Angry or Mad Feelings

Alexander and the Terrible, Horrible, No Good, Very Bad Day, by Judith Viorst (4–8)
Andrew's Angry Words, by Dorothea Lackner (4–8)
Bootsie Barker Bites, by Barbara Bottner (4–8)
The Chocolate-Covered-Cookie Tantrum, by Deborah Blementhal (5–8)
How I Feel Angry, by Marcia Leonard (infant–4)
How I Feel Frustrated, by Marcia Leonard (3–8)
Lily's Purple Plastic Purse, by Kevin Henkes (4–8)
The Rain Came Down, by David Shannon (4–8)
Sometimes I'm Bombaloo, by Rachel Vail (3–8)
That Makes Me Mad! by Steven Kroll (4–8)
The Three Grumpies, by Tamra Wight (4–8)
When I Feel Angry, by Cornelia Maude Spelman (5–7)
When I'm Angry, by Jane Aaron (3–7)
When Sophie Gets Angry—Really, Really Angry, by Molly Garrett (3–7)

Kid Books on Scared or Worried Feelings

Creepy Things Are Scaring Me, by Jerome and Jarrett Pumphrey (4–8)

Franklin in the Dark, by Paulette Bourgeois and Brenda Clark (5–8)

I Am Not Going to School Today, by Robie H. Harris (4–8)

No Such Thing, by Jackie French Koller (5–8)

Sam's First Day (in multiple languages), by David Mills and Lizzie Finlay (3–7)

Sheila Rae, the Brave, by Kevin Henkes (5–8)

Wemberly Worried, by Kevin Henkes (5–8)

When I Feel Scared, by Cornelia Maude Spelman (5–7)

Kid Books on Self-Confidence

ABC, I Like Me, by Nancy Carlson (4–6)

Amazing Grace, by Mary Hoffman (4–8)

Arthur's Nose, by Marc Brown (3–8)

The Blue Ribbon Day, by Katie Couric (4–8)

I Am Responsible! by David Parker (3–5)

I Can Do It Myself, by Emily Perl Kingsley (2–4)

I'm in Charge of Me! by David Parker (3–5)

The Little Engine That Could, by Watty Piper (3–7)

Susan Laughs, by Jeanne Willis (4–7)

Too Loud Lily, by Sophia Laguna (4–7)

Try and Stick with It, by Cheri Meiners (4–8)

26 Big Things Little Hands Can Do, by Coleen Paratore (1–6)

The Very Clumsy Click Beetle, by Eric Carle (3–7)

Whistle for Willie/Sebale a Willie, by Erza Jack Keats (4–7)

You Can Do It, Sam, by Amy Hest (2–6)

Kid Books on Behavior Expectations

Can You Listen with Your Eyes? by Nita Everly (6–7)

Can You Use a Good Voice? by Nita Everly (6–7)
David Gets in Trouble, by David Shannon (3–8)
David Goes to School, by David Shannon (3–8)
Excuse Me! A Little Book of Manners, by Karen Katz (infant–5)
Feet Are Not for Kicking (available in board book), by Elizabeth Verdick (2–4)
Hands Are Not for Hitting (available in board book), by Martine Agassi (2–8)
I Show Respect! by David Parker (3–5)
I Tell the Truth! by David Parker (3–5)
No Biting, by Karen Katz (infant–5)
No, David! by David Shannon (3–8)
No Hitting, by Karen Katz (infant–5)
Words Are Not for Hurting, by Elizabeth Verdick (3–6)

Kid Books on Family Relationships

Are You My Mother? by P. D. Eastman and Carlos Rivera (infant–5)
Baby Dance, by Ann Taylor (infant–4)
Counting Kisses, by Karen Katz (infant–5)
Don't Forget I Love You, by Miriam Moss (2–7)
Guess How Much I Love You, by Sam McBratney (infant–5)
Guji Guji, by Chih-Yuan Chen (5–8)
How Do I Love You? (available in board book) by P. K. Hallinan (infant–5)
I Love You: A Rebus Poem, by Jean Marzollo (1–6)
I Love You the Purplest, by Barbara M. Joose (4–8)
The Kissing Hand, by Audrey Penn (3–8)
Koala Lou, by Mem Fox (4–7)

Mama, Do You Love Me?/Me Quieres, Mama? by Barbara Joosse (3–6)

More, More, More, Said the Baby: Three Love Stories, by Vera B. Williams (infant–3)

Owl Babies, by Martin Waddell (3–7)

Please, Baby, Please, by Spike Lee (infant–5)

Te Amo Bebe, Little One, by Lisa Wheeler (infant–3)

You're All My Favorites, by Sam McBratney (5–7)

Kid Books on Problem Solving

Don't Let the Pigeon Drive the Bus! by Mo Willems (2–7)

Don't Let the Pigeon Stay Up Late! by Mo Willems (2–7)

I Did It, I'm Sorry, by Caralyn Buehner (5–8)

It Wasn't My Fault, by Helen Lester (4–7)

Talk and Work It Out, by Cheri Meiners (4–8)

Kid Books on Bullying and Teasing

The Berenstain Bears and the Bully, by Stan and Jan Berenstain (4–7)

Big Bad Bruce, by Bill Peet (4–8)

Chester's Way, by Kevin Henkes (5–7)

Coyote Raid in Cactus Canyon, by J. Arnosky (4–8)

Gobbles! by Ezra Jack Keats (4–8)

Hats, by Kevin Luthardt (3–6)

Hooway for Wodney Wat! by Helen Lester (5–8)

Hugo and the Bully Frogs, by Francesca Simon (3–7)

A Weekend with Wendell, by Kevin Henkes (4–8)

Kid Books on Grief and Death

The Fall of Freddie the Leaf, by Leo Buscaglia (5–adult)

Goodbye, Mousie, by Robi Harris (3–8)
I Miss You, by Pat Thomas (4–8)
The Next Place, by Warren Hanson (5–adult)
Sad Isn't Bad: A Good-Grief Guidebook for Kids Dealing with Loss, by Michaelene Mundy (5–8)

Positive Parenting Web Sites

Baby Center: www.babycenter.com
Building Blocks for a Healthy Future: www.bblocks.samhsa.gov
Center on the Social and Emotional Foundations for Early Learning (CSEFEL) www.vanderbilt.edu/csefel/
Child Welfare Information Gateway: www.childwelfare.gov
Fussy Baby Network: www.fussybabynetwork.org
The International Network for Children and Families (INCAF): www.incaf.com
National Association for the Education of Young Children: www.naeyc.org
Talaris Institute: www.Talaris.org
Zero to Three: www.zerotothree.org
Parent Training and Education The Basics of Nonviolent Communication (Marshall Rosen- berg): www.nonviolentcommunication.com
Brazelton Touchpoints Center: www.touchpoints.org
Center for Nonviolent Education and Parenting: www.cnvep.org
The Gottman Institute (Strengthen and repair marriages and relationships): www.gottman.com
The Incredible Years: www.incredibleyears.com

The International Network for Children and Families (IN-CAF): www.incaf.com

Nurturing Parenting: www.nurturingparenting.com

Parent Effectiveness Training: www.gordontraining.com

The Parent's Toolshop: The Universal Blueprint for Building a Healthy Family: www.parentstoolshop.com

About the Author

Kimberley Clayton Blaine, MA, LFMT, is a licensed child and family therapist, parenting expert, and advocate for neurodiversity and trauma-informed care. With over 30 years of experience, she helps families navigate complex diagnoses with compassion and science-based tools.

Founder of *TheMisunderstoodChild.com* and the **Clayton Blaine Scholarship for Preschool Teachers** at SDSU, Kimberley's award-winning books and programs have reached families worldwide, empowering parents to raise children who feel seen, safe, and understood. She is a published author with Jossey-Bass/Wiley, with her books reaching international audiences — including a best-selling parenting title in China.

Made in the USA
Coppell, TX
31 December 2025

67885574R00056